This book belongs to

_____

STERLING CHILDREN'S BOOKS
New York

An Imprint of Sterling Publishing
387 Park Avenue South
New York, NY 10016

Library of Congress Cataloging-in-Publication Data Available

Lot#:
2   4   6   8   10   9   7   5   3
09/12

Published by Sterling Publishing Co., Inc.
Text copyright © 2012 by The Book Shop, Ltd.
Illustrations copyright © 2012 by Troy Howell
Distributed in Canada by Sterling Publishing
c/o Canadian Manda Group, 165 Dufferin Street
Toronto, Ontario, Canada M6K 3H6
Distributed in the United Kingdom by GMC Distribution Services
Castle Place, 166 High Street, Lewes, East Sussex, England BN7 1XU
Distributed in Australia by Capricorn Link (Australia) Ptd. Ltd.
P.O. Box 704, Sindsor, NSW 2756, Australia

Printed in China

Sterling ISBN 978-1-4027-6454-7

For information about custom editions, special sales, premium and corporate purchases, please contact Sterling Special Sales Department at 800-805-5489 or specialsales@sterlingpublishing.com

First Prayers

TROY HOWELL

STERLING CHILDREN'S BOOKS
New York

Dear God,

Be good to me.

The sea is so wide

And my boat is so small.

PRAYER OF A FISHERMAN

All things bright and beautiful,
All creatures great and small,
All things wise and wonderful,
The Lord God made them all.

Each little flower that opens,
Each little bird that sings,
He made their glowing colors,
He made their tiny wings.

The tall trees in the greenwood,
The meadows where we play,
The rushes by the water
We gather every day—

He gave us eyes to see them,
And lips that we might tell,
How great is God Almighty,
Who has made all things well!

CECIL FRANCIS ALEXANDER

God made the world so broad and grand,
Filled with blessings from His hand.
He made the sky so high and blue;
He made the little children, too.

Unknown

This is the day which the Lord has made;
We will rejoice and be glad in it.

Psalm 118:24

North, South, East, and West,
May Thy holy name be blessed;
Everywhere beneath the sun,
May Thy holy will be done.

WILLIAM CANTON

Oh, the Lord is good to me,
And so I thank the Lord
For giving me the things I need:
The sun, the rain, and the apple seed.
Oh, the Lord is good to me.

ATTRIBUTED TO JOHN CHAPMAN
(JOHNNY APPLESEED)

These little hands are held in prayer
To thank you, God, for being there.
These little hearts speak to You,
To ask you, God, what we should do.
These little eyes are filled with love
For God in heaven up above.

UNKNOWN

He prayeth well, who loveth well
Both man and bird and beast.
He prayeth best, who loveth best
All things both great and small;
For the dear God who loveth us,
He made and loveth all.

SAMUEL TAYLOR COLERIDGE

Little Lamb, who made thee?
Dost thou know who made thee?
Gave thee life and bade thee feed
By the stream and over the mead;
Gave thee clothing of delight,
Softest clothing, woolly, bright;
Gave thee such a tender voice
Making all the vales rejoice?
Little lamb, who made thee?
Dost thou know who made thee?

Little lamb, I'll tell thee;

Little lamb, I'll tell thee;

He is called by thy name,

For He calls himself a Lamb;

He is meek and He is mild,

He became a little child.

I a child and thou a lamb,

We are called by His name,

Little lamb, God bless thee!

Little lamb, God bless thee!

WILLIAM BLAKE

Thank You for the world so sweet;
Thank You for the food we eat;
Thank You for the birds that sing;
Thank You, God, for everything!

EDITH RUTTER LEATHAM

For flowers that bloom about our feet,

Father, we thank Thee.

For tender grass so fresh and sweet,

Father, we thank Thee.

For the song of bird and hum of bee,

For all things fair we hear or see,

Father in heaven, we thank Thee.

For this new morning with its light,

Father, we thank Thee.

For rest and shelter of the night,

Father, we thank Thee.

For health and food, for love and friends,

For everything Thy goodness sends,

Father in heaven, we thank Thee.

RALPH WALDO EMERSON

Father, thank you for the night,
Thank you for the day,
For the chance to do some work,
And for the chance to play.

Thank you for my family,
Father, Mother, too,
Thank you for my playmates,
But most of all for You.

UNKNOWN

God bless all those that I love,
God bless all those that love me.
God bless all those that love those that I love,
And all those that love those that love me.

From an old New England sampler

I thank Thee, Lord, for Mom and Dad,
For rain and sunny weather.
I thank Thee, Lord, for all my friends
And that we are together.

Unknown

The little cares that fretted me,

I lost them yesterday

Among the fields above the sea,

Among the winds at play,

Among the lowing of the herds,

The rustling of the trees,

Among the singing of the birds,

The humming of the bees.

The foolish fears of what might pass,

I cast them all away

Among the clover-scented grass,

Among the new-mown hay,

Among the hushing of the corn,

Where drowsy poppies nod,

Where ill thoughts die and good are born—

Out in the fields with God.

Unknown

Lord, teach a little child to pray,
And then accept my prayer,
Thou hearest all the words I say
For Thou art everywhere.

A little sparrow cannot fall
Unnoticed, Lord, by Thee;
And though I am so young and small
Thou dost take care of me.

Teach me to do the thing that's right,
And when I sin, forgive;
And make it still my chief delight
To serve Thee while I live.

JANE TAYLOR

The year's at the spring
And day's at the morn;
Morning's at seven;
The hillside's dew-pearled;
The lark's on the wing;
The snail's on the thorn;
God's in His heaven—
All's right with the world!

ROBERT BROWNING

Now before I run to play,
Let me not forget to pray
To God who kept me through the night
And waked me with the morning light.

Help me, Lord, to love Thee more
Than I ever loved before,
In my work and in my play,
Be Thou with me through the day.

UNKNOWN

Father, we thank Thee for this food,
For health and strength and all things good.
May others all these blessings share,
And hearts be grateful everywhere.

UNKNOWN

Father in heaven, all through the night
I have been sleeping, safe in Thy sight.
Father, I thank Thee; bless me I pray,
Bless me and keep me all through the Day.

UNKNOWN

God bless the field and bless the furrow,

Stream and branch and rabbit burrow.

Bless the minnow; bless the whale.

Bless the rainbow and the hail.

Bless the nest, and bless the leaf.

Bless the righteous and the thief.

Bless the wing, and bless the fin.

Bless the air I travel in.

Bless the mill, and bless the mouse.

Bless the miller's red brick house.

Bless the earth, and bless the sea.

God bless you, and God bless me.

UNKNOWN

Jesus, tender shepherd, hear me;

Bless Thy little lamb tonight;

Through the darkness

Be Though near me,

Watch my sleep till morning light.

All this day Thy hand has led me,

And I thank Thee for Thy care;

Thou has warmed me and clothed

   and fed me;

Listen to my evening prayer.

MARY L DUNCAN

I see the moon,
And the moon sees me;
God bless the moon,
And God bless me.

UNKNOWN

Father, unto Thee I pray,
Thou hast guarded me all day;
Safe I am while in Thy sight,
Safely let me sleep tonight.

Bless my friends, the whole world bless;
Help me to learn helpfulness;
Keep me ever in Thy sight;
So to all I say good night.

HENRY JOHNSTONE

Lord, keep us safe this night,
Secure from all our fear;
May angels guard us while we sleep,
Till morning light appears.

JOHN LELAND

From ghoulies and ghosties,
Long-leggety beasties,
And things that go bump in the night,
Good Lord deliver us.

UNKNOWN

Index of First Lines